ALL ABOUT CRAPS

John Gollehon

A PERIGEE BOOK

Perigee Books
Published by
The Berkley Publishing Group
A division of Penguin Putnam Inc.
375 Hudson Street
New York, New York 10014

First Perigee edition 1988

Visit our website at
www.penguinputnam.com

ISBN 0-399-51462-7

Printed in the United States of America
35   34   33   32   31   30   29   28   27

CONTENTS

ALL ABOUT ABOUT CRAPS

CHAPTER 1

AN INTRODUCTION TO THE GAME

The origin of craps dates back to prehistoric times. According to some game historians, the actual dice were carved out of animal bone (presumably from a dinosaur), providing man's first game of chance.

Few players really care when the game was invented. I suppose it's possible that the same guy who invented the wheel, also invented craps. Besides, I have trouble visualizing a wild group of cavemen crowding a hot crap table.

Anyhow, the game is indeed old, and has had

plenty of time to stabilize. It reached its present-day identity in the early 1800's, introduced from Europe to New Orleans gambling halls.

So much for the history lesson. The important thing to conclude from all this is that craps, unlike other casino games, has reached a certain permanence. Where blackjack, for example, is continually changing as casino managers fine-tune the rules, craps remains essentially stable. *What you learn today will probably be true tomorrow, and for years to come.*

THE MOST EXCITING GAME IN THE CASINO!

Dice tables bring out the emotions more than any other game. There's a certain comradery among the players that for some reason doesn't occur as frequently at the other tables. Players feel free to yell, shout, scream, applaud, cheer, and let loose when they're winning. For the seasoned gambler, there are few things in life more exciting than a hot crap table. But it works both ways. Few things are more depressing than a cold table. The dice tables are a roller-coaster ride through the emotions; from sheer exuberance to the depths of despair.

High rollers like to play craps, and contribute to the game's "electricity" with their large bankroll. Sometimes, a table can win or lose hundreds of thousands of dollars in just a very short time. That fast! And that exciting!

Players and Watchers

In Las Vegas, especially during the summer months, the hotels fill their rooms with vacationers and convention guests, certainly not all experienced players. And in the evenings, these people roam the casino watching the games and the other players. When a crap table heats up, a large crowd usually gathers. The watchers can only wish they knew how to play, and wish they were up there with the players, sharing in the big profits.

For the inexperienced, watching a dice table can be a lot of fun. But how much more fun can it be to actually play?

Can you learn the game? Absolutely.
Is it easy? Very much so!
Can you win? Sure.
Can you lose? Of course.
Is there a big risk? Always.

But it can be fun. And for the disciplined player who can afford to gamble, exhibits self-control, and plays conservatively, the game probably won't hurt you, at least no more than slots. But remember, the dice tables are no place for reckless spenders. And the casino always has the advantage.

I can't guarantee that you'll win, or guarantee against loss. Obviously, no one can. And I'm not encouraging you to play if you have the slightest reservation. It's your decision.

Atlantic City

When Atlantic City casinos opened their doors in 1978, the number of craps players surprised even the most experienced casino managers (imported from Nevada). In each casino, the great majority of tables were blackjack, and only a few dice tables were installed. They took their cue from Nevada where a typical casino might have 30 blackjack tables and only six dice tables. In Nevada, that was the right ratio. But not in Atlantic City! The casinos soon realized that craps was a much more popular game in the East, and now the action is considered about even. Some casinos in New Jersey have over 30 dice tables!

An Easy Game To Learn And Play

The casual observer in a casino, who knows little if anything about casino games, would pick craps as the most complicated, difficult-to-learn game. Why? Because the table layout *looks* complicated. There are so many different types of bets. So much confusion. Sometimes 7 wins, and sometimes it loses. Unfortunately, many gamblers shy away from craps because they assume it's too difficult to master.

As any experienced dice player knows, the game is indeed simple. Perhaps the easiest to learn and play. More importantly, it's the most exciting game in the casino. But most important of all, craps offers certain wagers that give the house only a slight advantage. Some of the "best" bets you can make in a casino are at the dice table.

A COMPARISON WITH OTHER CASINO GAMES

A comparison of craps to the other casino games should give the reader a pretty good idea of what to expect. The worst games, in terms of casino advantage, are Keno and Slots. In the keno parlor (or in the casino's restaurants where keno boards are displayed) the player can figure to lose $1 for every $4 wagered. That represents a 25% game for the house and certainly no treat for any respectable player. Keno might *look* attractive with a $50,000 pay-off, and sure, you might get lucky; but your odds of winning are 230,114 to 1! Is it really worth it?

Slots are difficult to pin-point in terms of casino advantage, because the casino can set the percentages as they please. It's generally regarded that "downtown" Las Vegas casinos offer lower percentages than "strip" hotels, although there's no real documentation. However, some "win revenue" statements from big strip hotels indicate percentages fall around 10%. Again, that's too much to give away.

Baccarat experts claim that the casino advantage is less than 2%, but the casino's actual win revenue over a fiscal year supports a greater percentage. Besides, most casinos have a steep minimum betting level (the game appears to be reserved for high rollers) and there's reason to believe that the advantage is higher than most players think.

Next in order comes craps, with a variety of bets that can give the casino an advantage from .8% (that's point-eight) to over 16%. If the player only makes bets that keep the house percentage to a minimum, then craps is a relatively low percentage game. Not bad.

Blackjack is indeed the best in terms of casino advantage, because the percentages are constantly changing. Sometimes, the player can acquire a significant advantage! However, only a master-counter can detect these changes and alter his playing strategy and betting levels accordingly.

So there you have it. Craps is better than most games, except blackjack, and is considerably easier to learn and play. But at no time does the player acquire an edge.

CHAPTER 2

HOW TO PLAY

To understand the game, let's first consider the dice. There are two dice in play, with each cube having six sides, 1 through 6. That means that numbers from 2 through 12 can appear when two dice are thrown.

Let's make an important distinction right now. *The probability of each number varies.* They are not all the same. Your chances of rolling a 4 are much less than rolling a 7. We'll get into that in specific detail later in this chapter, but for now, it's important that you realize this fact from the outset.

THE PASS-LINE BET

Let's list the numbers somewhat out-of-order, so you can best see what the numbers mean for the most common dice wager—the "pass-line" bet. Here are the numbers in groups for you to study. Always think of the numbers exactly as I've separated them.

2-3-12	7-11	4-10	5-9	6-8
Craps (loser)	Natural (winner)	Point Numbers (must be repeated to win)		

Each of the numbers: 2, 3, and 12 is called a "craps," and it's a loser. 7 and 11 are called a "natural," and it's a winner. The remaining numbers: 4, 5, 6, 8, 9, and 10 are called "point-numbers," and must be *repeated* before a 7 is rolled in order to win.

When a player is handed the dice to throw, the first roll is called a "come-out," and a 7 or 11 immediately wins. The 2, 3, or 12 immediately loses. If the player throws any of the other numbers: 4, 5, 6, 8, 9, or 10 . . . there is no decision yet.

The player continues to throw the dice until either that same point-number is rolled again (in which case the player wins), or until a 7 is rolled (in which case the player loses). Any other number has no significance to the pass-line wager.

Now you can see why the 7 sometimes wins, and sometimes loses. If it's thrown on the first roll, it wins. But if it's thrown while the player is trying to repeat his point-number, the 7 loses. And that's called a "seven-out."

The dice then pass to the next player, and it's his turn to shoot. As long as the shooter continues to make passes (wins), either on the come-out immediately with a 7 or 11, or by repeating the point successfully, he retains the dice. The player keeps the dice even if he loses on the come-out roll with a 2, 3, or 12. *The player only loses the dice when he sevens-out.*

What we've just described is a pass-line bet, the heart of craps, and the most widely made bet at the table.

Now, let's pretend to walk up to the table. Look at the illustration of the table layout. Notice the area marked "Pass-Line." That's where the pass-line wager is made. Place your bet in that part of the pass-line area that's *directly in front of you*.

Also notice that the pass-line extends around both ends of the table. And notice that in fact, *both ends of the table are identical.* For now, don't pay any attention to the rest of the layout.

Follow the "Puck"

How do you know if the shooter is "coming-out" or trying to repeat his point-number? It's

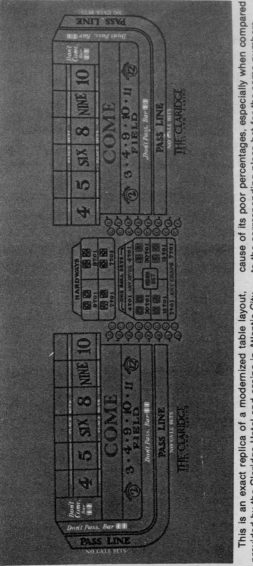

This is an exact replica of a modernized table layout, provided by the Claridge Hotel and casino in Atlantic City. Notice that the new layout gives the correct odds expressions for the prop bets, such as 7 to 1, instead of 8 "for" 1, long considered a deceitful tactic on older style layouts.

In addition, the new design does not include the big 6 or 8 on the corners, a bet that might become extinct be-

cause of its poor percentages, especially when compared to the corresponding place bet for the same numbers.

Other bets becoming increasingly unpopular among skilled players are the one-roll propositions such as any-7 and field bets. Since field bets appeal to the inexperienced player, giving over 5½% to the house, they are not recommended or discussed in this text.

easy. The first thing to notice on the table is a round 3¾ ″ diameter "puck" that says "ON" on one side, and "OFF" on the other. The "ON" side is white, and the "OFF" side is black. Where this puck is located will tell you the stage of the game when you walk up.

Look at the table illustration again, and notice the big boxes at the back of the table that represent point-numbers. There's a set of boxes for both ends of the table. There's a box for the 4, 5, 6, 8, 9, and 10. If the shooter made a point on the come-out roll, and is now trying to repeat that number, that's where the dealers will place the puck. Towards the rear center of the correct box.

When the puck is placed in one of the point boxes, the white side (ON) is up. If the puck is in the box marked "six," that's the point-number the shooter is after.

If the puck is noticed with the black side (OFF) showing, it's usually placed in an adjacent box marked "Don't-Come," and that means the next roll is a come-out.

In Northern Nevada, the don't-come box is in a different spot for some reason, so the puck is placed directly beside (not in) the point box nearest to the end of the table. The puck is nearest to the 4-box on the left side of the table, and nearest to the 10-box on the right side.

As you might imagine, it usually takes more time for a shooter to try and repeat a point-number than to throw a craps or natural on the come-out roll. So, at that instant you walk up to the table, the shooter will probably be going for his point-number. Possibly, you timed it perfectly and the shooter is about to make his come-out roll.

That's your signal to make a pass-line wager. Incidentally, **never make a pass-line bet while the shooter is trying for a point,** because then it's a bad bet. We'll tell you why later in the chapter.

When the shooter wins, everyone on the pass-line wins! Unlike "street" craps, all the players at the dice table are playing against the house, not each other.

YOU MUST KNOW THE ODDS!

The next bet we must learn is called an "odds-bet," and it's directly associated with the pass-line bet that we now know how to make. But before we can understand the odds-bet, we have to learn what "odds" means, and what the correct odds are at a dice table for all the possible numbers. Study the following chart for a moment, and you'll soon learn the probability of rolling any particular number.

NUMBER	WAYS	PROBABILITY	HOW
2	1	35 to 1	1-1
3	2	17 to 1	1-2, 2-1
4	3	11 to 1	2-2, 1-3, 3-1
5	4	8 to 1	1-4, 4-1, 2-3, 3-2
6	5	6.2 to 1	3-3, 2-4, 4-2, 1-5, 5-1
7	6	5 to 1	1-6, 6-1, 2-5, 5-2, 3-4, 4-3
8	5	6.2 to 1	4-4, 2-6, 6-2, 3-5, 5-3
9	4	8 to 1	3-6, 6-3, 4-5, 5-4
10	3	11 to 1	5-5, 4-6, 6-4
11	2	17 to 1	5-6, 6-5
12	1	35 to 1	6-6
	36		

In this chart, it's readily apparent that there are more ways to roll a 7 than any other number. "Probability" means the same as odds, and it's easy to compute if you have to.

We know there are 36 ways to roll the dice. And we know there are six ways to roll a 7. That means there must be 30 ways to *not* roll a 7 (36 - 6). So our odds of rolling the seven are 30 to 6. Dividing both numbers by 6 gives us 5 to 1.

THE ODDS OF ROLLING A 7:

WILL NOT HAPPEN—(5) TO (1)—WILL HAPPEN
        └ + ┘——TOTAL NUMBER OF TRIALS

Out of six rolls, one roll should be a 7; five rolls should be some other number. *That's 5 to 1 odds.* Notice that I said "should be." It's not an absolute. It's an absolute probability.

The actual results may deviate somewhat over the *short term,* and that's what a skilled player is looking for. *An opportunity when the odds have wavered.* But, over the *long term,* a 7 will come up once for every six rolls. Never argue with the laws of probability.

Who Has the Advantage?

Now that we understand odds at the dice table, let's go back to the pass-line rules and see how we stand. Let's see who has the advantage.

OK, we know there are four ways to throw a craps, and eight ways to make a 7 or 11. Wait a minute! We have an edge here! You bet we do! *The player always has a strong advantage on the come-out roll.*

There must be a catch. And there is. The point-numbers! When the shooter has established a point, the casino gets the edge. Again, it's easy to see why.

There are six ways to make the 7, and remember the 7 loses when a point-number has been established. No other point-number can be made *six* ways. Your best chance of rolling a point-number before a 7 is obviously a 6 or 8, since both numbers can be made *five* ways. But the 7 is more likely.

That's why we said earlier never to make a pass-line bet when the shooter has established a point-number. That's a dumb bet! You're giving up the best part of the pass-line wager—the come-out roll whcrc you have an edge, and you're getting down just at the time when the casino gets the nod. Not too smart!

The next logical question is who has the edge when you take *both* the come-out and point-numbers into account? Not surprisingly, the casino still gets the prize, but not by much. The casino advantage all-total, is 1.41%.

A Problem for You to Solve

The best way to fully grasp the probabilities of dice is to work out a problem on your own. Let me give you an easy problem to work on, all by yourself, and with the aid of our Probability Chart.

What are the odds that a shooter will throw a point-number on the come-out roll? Your answer will yield an important probability to always remember.

Here's how we find it. We know there are 36 ways to roll the dice, right? And all the ways to throw only a point-number are 24.

POINT NUMBERS	WAYS EACH	TOTAL WAYS
6 & 8	5	10
5 & 9	4	8
4 & 10	3	6
		24

If we subtract the number of ways to make a point-number, 24, from the total ways for all numbers, 36, we have 12 . . . which obviously is the total number of ways *not* to make a point-number. So, 12 to 24 is easily reduced to 1 to 2. That's our answer!

ODDS EXPRESSED AS A PERCENTAGE

When odds are expressed as 1 to 2, it means that in three trials to make an event happen, one time it won't happen, and two times it will. If we wish to express the odds as a percentage, as is often done, we simply divide the number of times the event *will happen* according to the odds, by the total number of trials (the total of both numbers in the odds expression).

In this case, we divide 2 by 3. That's the fraction 2/3 (fractions are still another way to express probabilities) and a percentage of 66%. *A 66% chance that our shooter will indeed make a point-number on the come-out roll.*

1 TO 2 ODDS EXPRESSED AS A FRACTION, NUMBER, PERCENTAGE:

$$\frac{\text{NUMBER OF TIMES AN EVENT WILL HAPPEN}}{\text{TOTAL NUMBER OF TRIALS*}} = \frac{2}{3} = .666 = 66.6\%$$

*The total of both numbers in the odds expression.

Yet a third way to express a probability, and technically we've already performed it, is with a number between 0 and 1. If an event can't possibly happen, the number is 0. If the event is positively bound to happen, the number is 1. In between are all the decimal numbers such as .666 (nothing more than the fraction expressed as a decimal).

You'll be happy to know that there are no other ways to express a probability that I know of. If there are any, I don't want to hear about it.

Readers who are learning from "scratch" may accuse me of writing a "trick" question, because the numbers appear to be turned around. Always remember that the first number represents the event *not happening*. Based on the way I purposely phrased the question, the answer of 1 to 2 is correct.

The first number (1), is smaller than the second number (2), because the odds are greater than even (1 to 1) that the event *will* happen.

If the likelihood of the event happening is less than even, as is more often the case, then the odds are obviously expressed with the larger number first.

If the question would have been phrased, "What are the odds that a shooter *will not* throw a point-number on the come-out roll," then the correct answer would have been 2 to 1, because the likelihood of the shooter *not* making a point-number is less than even.

Always Remember Point-Numbers in Pairs

You should now be able to see why we combined the point-numbers in our earlier chart . . . 6&8, 5&9, 4&10. Because the ways are the *same* for both numbers in each pair. Accordingly, when odds are computed for any point-number, it's always the same for the corresponding number in the pair.

Remember the point-numbers in pairs. That's important.

THE ODDS-BET

Now that we really understand odds, we can learn how to make the important odds-bet. *This wager is made only when the shooter has established a point.* Place the odds-bet directly behind the pass-line bet, but out of the pass-line area. The casino will allow you to bet an amount equal to your pass-line wager (single-odds) or double the amount of your pass-line bet if double-odds are offered. We'll see later in this chapter that double-odds is a big advantage to the player, so look for the casino that offers it.

What's nice about the odds-bet is that the casino will pay you correct odds on that bet, as opposed to the pass-line wager that pays even money (1 to 1).

Here's a chart that gives you the correct odds of the point-numbers being repeated before a 7 is rolled. It's important that you *remember these odds* because it tells you how you will be paid if you win.

POINT NUMBER	CORRECT ODDS OF REPEATING BEFORE A 7
6-8	6 to 5
5-9	3 to 2
4-10	2 to 1

Let's say the shooter established 4 as his point. If you have $5 bet on the pass-line, you can make an odds-bet of $5 (or $10 at a double-odds table). If the shooter successfully repeats the 4, you will be paid $5, even money, for the pass-line bet of $5, and 2 to 1 for your $5 odds-bet which is $10! (or $20 if you took $10 double-odds).

Since the casino pays off the odds-bet at correct odds, there is absolutely no casino advantage. In fact, the odds-bet is the only bet you can make in the casino that can be determined mathematically to have no advantage either to the player or to the casino. Over the long term, you'll neither win nor lose on your odds-bet wagers.

It's easy to prove that the odds-bet is indeed a fair bet. If the odds are 2 to 1 that a 7 will be rolled before a 4, then the payoff is correct, and the bet yields no advantage to the casino or player. We can compute from the earlier chart in this chapter that there are six ways to roll a 7, and three ways to roll a 4. 6 to 3 reduces to 2 to 1. Since the casino pays off at 2 to 1, they have no advantage.

Logically, you might ask why make such a big deal about a bet that only "evens out" over a long term. Let me answer your question with my own question. Would you rather make bets that *always* give the casino a rock-solid advantage, or would you prefer a bet that's truly a fair game? A bet in the casino that doesn't favor the house, *is* a big deal!

The Odds-Bet Reduces the Casino Advantage

Making the odds-bet along with the pass-line wager reduces the casino's total pass-line advantage from 1.4% to about .85%. Double-odds reduces the house edge even more to about .63%! True, you're risking more money to earn a lower house percentage, but it's strongly recommended.

Although the double-odds bet does not directly affect the house percentage on the pass-line part of the wager, it does lower the percentage for the *total amount of your wager*. And in reality, that's what we're concerned about.

The key to using double-odds sensibly is in the way you "size" your bets. Let's compare a pass-line wager of $15 with no odds to another pass-line bet of $5 with $10 in odds. If the point is 4, you would be paid only $15 in winnings for the $15 pass-line wager, compared to $25 for the $5 pass-line bet with $10 odds. See? It depends on how you structure your bets to earn the advantage of double-odds without increasing your total risk.

The Odds-Bet Must be a Proper Amount

Most players have little difficulty understanding single or double-odds, and regularly make the odds-bets as they should.

The problem usually comes in betting the proper amount in order to be paid correctly. Here's an example.

If the player has a $5 line bet and the point-number is 5, it seems perfectly proper to make a $5 odds-bet, right?

Wrong! How can the casino correctly pay off the odds-bet if it wins? 3 to 2 odds means the casino will pay $3 to every $2 wagered. Two goes into $5 two and a half times, multiplied times three is $7.50. A bit elementary but that's the way to think it through.

But, there are no half-dollars at the crap tables! A silver dollar (or $1 chip) is the smallest they have. *Always make sure the payoff is possible for the casino using $1 as the minimum divisible value.*

But what if you only wanted to bet $5 on the line? That's fine. If the point is 5 or 9, the casino will allow you to increase your odds-bet wager to $6. You'll get 3 to 2 for your $6 which correctly pays off a nice $9.00. Incidentally, the dealer will probably give you two red chips (a red chip is $5) and take away one dollar from your original bet.

Of course, with double-odds you would have bet $10 as odds and been paid $15 if the 5 or 9 repeated.

Just be sure the correct payoff never includes a fraction of a dollar. And to do that, you have to know what the odds really are.

Look at the chart again. *Think 6 to 5 for 6&8, 3 to 2 for 5&9, and 2 to 1 for the end numbers 4&10.* After a while, you'll know these simple odds as well as you know your own name.

By the way, don't think that payoffs are a problem just with small wagers. A $25 line bet with $25 odds for the points 5 or 9 can't be paid correctly either. You may go to the next unit value which is $30 to insure a correct odds payoff. Odds-bets with 5 or 9 the point, must be divisible by two. Similarly, odds-bets for the points 6 and 8 must be divisible by five. Points 4 and 10 are no problem since they pay 2 to 1. And everything is divisible by one!

Most players unfortunately make these mistakes because they have no inkling what the odds are. If they win, they're happy. *They don't realize they've just been shorted!*

The Odds-Bet is Easiest at Double-Odds Table

Since the size of your odds-bet seems to be the most confusing issue with new players, let's stay with it for a moment.

The easiest way to make sure your odds-bet can be paid at correct odds, is to play only at a double-odds table, with a red chip ($5) minimum pass-line wager, or any multiple of the red chip . . . two, three, four red chips and so on.

Of course, it also works for a green chip or black chip. Green chips are $25 and black chips are $100, but that's a little steep to start with.

Assuming you begin play with red chips as I do, any odds-bet you make will be double any multiple of $5, and *divisible by both two and five*. It works. Take my word for it.

Incidentally, the casino term for the amount of your pass-line bet is called a "flat" wager. At the double-odds table, simply bet double the amount of your flat wager. It's that simple. You've made the right bet. You've reduced the casino advantage as low as you can. And you know your bet can be paid correctly if you play as most players do, with red chips.

It's a good rule to remember, and a safe betting amount to begin with. Red chips aren't "chopped liver." You can easily work your way up to a total wager of $90 in red chips, $30/$60, accumulate a few "greenies" in your payoffs, and feasibly win over a thousand in just a few rolls.

By the way, never be intimidated by the player next to you who's betting thousands at a crack. There's absolutely nothing wrong with red chips! Pay attention to your own bets, and be content with your "red" action.

Later on, we'll learn how to properly, and safely, press-up your bets as the opportunity arises, but only when you're ahead and winning!

Make the Most of Your Odds-Bets!

There's only one drawback to what we've just covered, and that's the fact that most casinos only offer *single-odds*. Fortunately, more and more casinos are changing over to double-odds, but what can we do to increase our odds-bet at the *single-odds table*, if that's the only table we can find? Remember that your odds-bet at a single-odds table is usually limited to the amount of your flat wager on the pass-line.

Actually, there are two ways to increase your odds-bet if you're stuck at a single-odds table. And we've already discussed one of them earlier. If you recall, the casino will allow you to increase the odds-bet by a minimum amount to insure that your bet can be paid correctly.

In addition, the casino will also allow you to increase the size of your odds-bet to insure that payoffs will always be in chip values that are the *same or larger* than the value of chips you have wagered on the pass-line.

Here's an example. Suppose your pass-line bet is $30. If you made an odds-bet of $30 and won on a point of 6 or 8, you would be paid $36. Somewhere in there is a silver dollar. If you won on $40, your payoff is $48. A payoff of red, green, and silver dollars.

As a courtesy to the players (that's the casino's reason), they allow the pass-line wager of $30 to $45 to take an odds wager of $50. That's the next multiple of $5 chips that will yield a payoff that can be made *without* silver dollars. Most casinos now use casino-issued silver dollars instead of $1 chips—too expensive to manufacture. The fake silver dollars are usually good in other casinos unlike chips, with the theory they're worth at least a dollar in metal. But don't try to use them back home. The MGM lion doesn't go over as well as Eisenhower at your friendly bank.

To push the point home about making this bet . . . here's one more example. Say your pass-line bet is $100 . . . four green chips. If the point is 6 or 8, the casino will allow five green chips as the odds-bet. That makes the payoff easy. Six green chips to the *five* green chips wagered. No red, all green. Got it?

The Three-Unit Wager

When I play at a single-odds table, I make it a rule to always bet three chips on the pass-line. Here's why.

The casino will allow an odds-bet of five chips for the points 6 and 8, four chips for the points 5 and 9, and a flat wager of three chips for the points 4 and 10. That's especially nice because my winning payoff will always be *nine chips*. If the payoff is ever less than nine chips, the dealer mis-paid me and I won't pick them up until he sees the discrepency. Dealers do on rare occasion make a mistake. But not very often. Here's the "three-unit" bet rule to remember.

POINT	PASS-LINE	ODDS-BET	PAYOFF
6 & 8	3 chips	5 chips	9 chips
5 & 9	3 chips	4 chips	9 chips
4 & 10	3 chips	3 chips	9 chips

The bet is allowed, as we said before, as a courtesy to the player so that all winning payoffs are in chip values of your wager (or more, not less). Regardless, it's a way to increase your odds bet, especially when 6 or 8 is the point. Three red chips, three green chips, or three black chips . . . always try to make the three-unit wager at the single-odds tables.

THE COME-BET

The come-bet is best described as a "delayed" pass-line wager. And there's no question where to place it. The largest block of the table is assigned for a come-bet. The area has the name "COME" boldly displayed.

If you make a come-bet by placing a chip in that area *near your position at the table,* it's the same as a pass-line bet except that you're making the bet *while the shooter is trying to repeat a point-number*. That's the only time you can make a come-bet, otherwise the bet would obviously be placed on the pass-line since the bet is exactly the same.

Let's say the shooter's number to win on the pass-line has been established as 6. If you wish to have another bet working in addition to the pass-line, simply make a come-bet as I've described. If the next roll is a 9, you'll be looking for another 6 or 9 (before a 7) to win either bet. It can be said that you have two numbers "working" . . . 6 "on the line" and 9 "coming."

Had the next roll been a craps, you would have lost the come-bet. A 7 or 11 would have won outright, but remember, the 7 would have wiped out the pass-line. Mixed emotions!

When a 7 or 11 is rolled on a come-bet, the dealer immediately places the payoff directly beside your bet. It's your responsibility to *immediately* pick up the chips, otherwise the bet "works" on the next roll as another come-bet. On the other hand, if a craps is thrown, the dealer simply picks up your chip, and it's up to you to make another bet.

The Point-Box

Assuming the roll is a point-number, your come-bet does not remain in the come area. *The dealer will reposition your bet in the numbered boxes for the point-numbers in a spot that's directly refer-*

enced to your location at the table.

If you're standing at the corner of the table, the come-bet will be moved to the corner of the point-box. That's how the dealer (and you) can keep track of your bets and distinguish them from other come-bets in the same point-box made by other players.

You'll want to make an odds-bet along with your come-bet when it goes to a point-box, for the same reason you must make the odds-bet behind your pass-line wagers when a point is established. Remember, it lowers the casino advantage considerably!

How to Make an Odds-Bet on the Come

To make an odds-bet in the come area, simply position the bet near the original come-bet and announce to the dealer loudly and clearly, "Odds on my come-bet." Do not place the odds chips on top of your come-bet, for obvious reasons. You recall, I hope, that the odds-bet is paid at correct odds whereby the come-bet (flat wager) is paid only at even money. You *must* keep the chips separate.

When the come-bet and odds-bet are repositioned in the point-box, the dealer places the odds wager on top of the come-bet, but *slightly offset* to distinguish the two different bets. Always watch the dealer to be sure he understood you and in fact, has your bets positioned correctly, and in the proper location.

When the shooter repeats a come-bet point-number for you, the dealer will immediately return your come-bet and odds-bet to the come area where you originally placed them.

Next, he'll place your winning chips directly beside the bet, for you to pick up. Again, if you don't pick up all the chips, they work on the next roll as another come-bet. Be careful!

Incidentally, when you make a come-bet and odds-bet, always be sure to position the bets in the come area *near the perimeter and in direct line with where you're standing*. Don't throw your chips or place them just anywhere in the come area.

Your bet may later be confused with another come-bet placed by another player. It's your responsibility to keep track of your own chips. There's always some jerk at the table who thinks *your* chips are *his* chips.

Why Make Come-Bets?

The best reason I can give you for making come-bets is to gang-up on the table when a shooter is repeating a lot of point-numbers that would otherwise be useless to you. Don't let all those beautiful point-numbers go to waste! That's your cue to make lots and lots of come-bets.

I've seen many instances when a shooter rolled the dice for more than a half-hour before he finally sevened-out. How nice!

Off and On

You can make as many come-bets as you want to. And when the shooter is throwing numbers, and numbers, and numbers . . . enjoy yourself! Frequently, you might have all five remaining point-numbers covered with come-bets. Quite often, the shooter will roll a point-number that you already have covered with a come-bet.

When this happens, the action is termed "OFF AND ON," meaning the dealer will simply pay your "net" winnings as if the chips moved about on the table as they normally would. Unnecessary actions.

The net result, if you stop and think about it, is that you win the come-bet with odds in the point-box, so that's what the dealer will pay you, directly beside your last come-bet. Pick it up and leave the last come-bet to work again for you. Your original come-bet with odds (on which you were actually paid) will also stay where it is in the point-box, waiting for another *off and on* payoff.

Off On the Come

The player may remove his odds-bet wagers any time, or simply call the bets "off" whenever he likes, on a whim or whatever. Although there's no particularly good reason for doing it.

Of course, the player can't remove a pass-line or come-bet. Otherwise, the player would have a healthy advantage, as we told you earlier by just letting the bet work on the come-out (where the player has a big advantage) and then simply taking the bet down if a point-number is established (where the edge swings to the casino). Obviously, the casino won't go for that!

But, since the odds-bet is fair, no advantage either way, the casino will let you do as you please with it.

They do however, have a standing rule that all odds-bets are automatically *off* on the come-out unless the player says otherwise (that they're working). The theory is that most players don't want to lose the odds-bets in case a 7 is rolled on the come-out which would wipe out all the come-bets placed in the point-boxes. The 7 will in fact wipe out your come-bets, but with the odds called off, the dealer will return all your odds-bets to you. It's a standard house rule, so go with it.

ONLY THREE BETS TO REMEMBER

We've just learned the pass-line bet, odds-bet, and come-bet in a manner that may have seemed a bit lengthy to you, especially if you're an experienced player. Sure, I could have reviewed the bets in two or three paragraphs . . . just like the casinos do for you in their little gaming booklets you can get free for the asking.

Purposely, I repeated important aspects of making these bets to help you remember them. Purposely, I went through it slowly with you, using many examples, to make sure you know exactly what to do, and exactly why you're doing it.

This is not a crash course. If you want a succinct explanation of craps, get the free booklet from the casino. But don't look for the bets *not* to make, or any mention of casino percentages. Don't look for fine details as I've given you. You'll learn how to play and you'll learn how to lose. You get what you pay for.

We've spent a lot of time on three particular bets that you can make at a dice table because frankly, **there are no other bets that you really need to know about.** Sure there are lots of other bets to make. But none are as favorable to you as the three bets we've concentrated on. Technically, you should stop right now, review the previous pages, and go play.

I hesitate to tell you about all the other bets you can make at a craps table, for fear you *will* make them. You shouldn't! But to make this chapter complete, here's a brief rundown of all the other bets. Brief indeed, because there's no reason to concentrate on any of them. If you forget them, that's better yet. Here goes.

PLACE BETS

For the player who's too anxious to get his money on the table, the casino will allow a bettor to "place" any or all of the point-numbers without having to go through the rigamarole of waiting for them to come up as a come-bettor must do.

But for this "luxury," you have to pay a price. Certainly, the casino won't pay correct odds as they do on your odds-bet. No way! Here's a schedule of how the casino pays place bets. Note the casino advantages compared to .63% on the pass-line and come.

PLACE NUMBER	ODDS PAYOFF	SHOULD BE	CASINO ADVANTAGE
6-8	7 to 6	6 to 5	1.52%
5-9	7 to 5	3 to 2	4%
4-10	9 to 5	2 to 1	6.67%

Granted, placing the 6 or 8 is not that bad, 1.52% to the house. Occasionally, I'll catch myself placing a 6 or 8 if the number's not covered with a come-bet. Still, the casino edge is *two and a half times greater* than a pass-line or come-bet with double-odds. It shouldn't be recommended.

In the event you *do* place a 6 or 8, be sure to make your wager in multiples of six dollars, or six chips, because the payoff is 7 to every 6 you've wagered. For instance, if you bet $30 on the 6, the payoff is $35.

Certainly you can see why placing the 5 or 9 is a poor wager. Indeed, placing the 4 or 10 is totally ludicrous. If you're dead-set on getting immediate action on those numbers, at least "buy" the 4 or 10. That's the next bet to talk about.

THE BUY BET

For some reason, the casino will give you an option on placing the point-numbers. You can either place them as we've discussed, or you can "buy" them.

If you buy the number, the casino will pay you the correct odds, just like on the odds-bet. But they charge you a 5% commission to do this.

Since the casino edge on the points 5, 9, 6, and 8 is less than 5%, it would be stupid to buy these numbers. But on the points 4 and 10, 5% is obviously lower than 6.67% (the place bet percentage) so it does pay to buy the 4 or 10 instead of placing it.

So, if in your "expert opinion," a whole bunch of 4's and 10's are about to be rolled, go ahead and buy 'em. For every green chip you wager, the dealer will give you two.

I mention the green chip because 5% of $25 is $1.25, but the casino will settle for $1 even. Don't make the buy bet for less than $20 however, because the minimum commission is $1 (the smallest chip at most tables).

Technically, the casino advantage is a little less than 5%, but it's close enough.

PROP BETS

Our Chapter on craps cannot be finished without a discussion of "prop" bets, but believe me, *you will be finished* if you make them!

Prop is short for "proposition," and that's the name of all these neat little bets you can make in the center layout of the table.

Each prop bet represents a "teardrop" on the casino's chandeliers. Remember that!

The bets are either a one-roll decision or "hardway." If you make a bet on the "hard-six," you win if the number comes up 3-3, and lose if the 6 comes up any *other* way, or with a 7. The accompanying chart details all the prop bets and gives the casino advantages. The heading is appropriate.

DUMBEST BETS AT THE DICE TABLE

BET	PAYS	SHOULD PAY	CASINO ADVANTAGE
Any-7	4 to 1	5 to 1	16.67% (Wow!)
Any Craps	7 to 1	8 to 1	11.1%
11 (or 3)	15 to 1	17 to 1	11.1%
2 (or 12)	30 to 1	35 to 1	13.89%
Hard 6 (or 8)	9 to 1	10 to 1	9.1%
Hard 4 (or 10)	7 to 1	8 to 1	11.1%

On some table layouts, the prop payoffs will be "disguised" as *correct* payoffs such as 8 for 1 on the hard 4 or 10. Sounds like correct odds, right?

Wrong! "For" means you don't keep your bet. "To" does. 8 for 1 is the same as 7 to 1. Don't be misled by the casino's cheap tactic.

DON'T PASS, DON'T COME, AND DON'T GET EXCITED

The areas of the table layout marked DON'T PASS and DON'T COME are for betting "with" the casino, and against all the other players, assuming they're not all making "don't" bets with you.

If the shooter doesn't make his point, you win, just like the casino. A craps roll on the come-out wins instead of loses, however the casino calls it a "push" on the craps-12. "Push" means no action . . . a standoff.

The casino advantage is about as small as the "right" side (betting the dice *do* pass) and the BAR-12 as the push is called, counts more than you think towards the casino's advantage.

The only problem with the "don't" bets is that you want a cold table to win. You're siding with the enemy.

I never play the "don't" side because it's too damn boring. No excitement. Which reminds me. Never yell and scream and wave your arms when you win because the shooter sevened-out. Other players may have lost thousands! You'll get "looks that could kill!'' Be sure a security guard is handy if you plan on touting your win to the other players.

If you're the type who likes to antagonize other people, the ''don't'' bets were designed just for you.

CHAPTER 3

THE EQUIPMENT—TABLE, DICE, AND CREW

Now that we understand how craps is played, let's delve into more detail about the table itself, and the crew that works it.

The game is so basic, that technically we really don't need the table! In the good ol' army days, or in the Bowery, players simply threw the dice against a wall . . . any wall. A building would do, or even a curb. The "table" might have been a sidewalk or a lonely alley. Of course, the casinos won't let you play dice on their sidewalks. That would interfere with valet parking. For the sake of accuracy and organization, the casinos provide tables.

THE TABLE

Casino craps tables are elaborate pieces of furniture costing thousands of dollars. In Nevada, there are three different sizes of tables in use, allowing up to 14, 16, and 18 players. The shorter tables are not widely used, although preferred by many experienced players. In Las Vegas, Caesar's Palace uses the short tables, while across the street at the Dunes you can find the longest ones.

At the longer tables, if you're standing at one end and the dice are tossed to the other end, you might need binoculars to read the numbers!

Another problem with the longer tables is the frequency of the dice bouncing off the table. The shooter must bounce the dice off the wall at the opposite end of the table from where he's standing. The longer tables require a longer toss (a harder throw) and "too tall" (off the table) calls are common.

Some players believe that the long tables create problems for the dealers too, especially when the table's full and the dice are passing. There are more players to pay off on each roll of the dice, more confusion, and at the very least, a slow-up of the game.

Personally, I like the short tables at Caesar's so

I play there frequently. There's more intimacy around a smaller table and I can see the other end! Incidentally, regardless of the table's size, I always position myself next to the stickman near the center of the table; I never play at a far end. There's a special reason for this rule that many experienced players also heed. *At that position, there are four members of the crew that should hear my instructions: the dealer, the stickman, and both boxmen.* Towards the end of the table, only the dealer is in communication with a player, and any dispute can be difficult to settle. And there *are* disputes! As impressed as I am with most dice dealers and their ability to handle pay-offs with incredible accuracy, occasionally there's a mistake. And most times, it's a mistake in communication.

The Layout Helps Keep Bets Separate

Regardless of the table's length, the layouts are all alike. Having a layout helps to identify each player's bet, and keeps those bets separate from other players. *It's important that a beginning player learns how and where the dealer positions his bets* (those that the player does not position himself such as the pass-line). Both come-bets and place bets are positioned in the point boxes based on the player's relative position around the table. Here's the way it works. *The front line (side) of each point box represents the front row of players,* between the stickman and the corner of the table. *The back line of each point box refers to the player's position from the corner of the table to the dealer* (the end sections of the table). The corner of the table represents the corner of the point box. Only the front and back sides of the point boxes are used when positioning your bets.

The longer tables have wider point boxes to allow extra room for the additional players and their corresponding bets that might go to the boxes. If in doubt about your point box position, simply ask the dealer. He'll point it out exactly for you. And always remember to watch your bets carefully, especially those in the point boxes. It's *your* money!

THE CREW

Each table is assigned a crew of four dealers, although only three are actually working the table at a given time. The other dealer is on "break." The dealers rotate positions by working 40 minutes "on base" at one of the two ends of the table, then their break, followed by 20 minutes "on the stick." When on base, they are handling the bets of all players at their end of the table. When on the stick, the dealer is in charge of the prop bets at the center of the table, presents the dice to the shooter, and calls the rolls. Since the dealer uses a curved stick to retrieve the dice for the shooter, the term "stickman" is commonly used. However, since the player must give instructions to the dealers and the stickman from time to time, it's recommended that the player reads the dealer's name on his breast-badge, and uses it. Don't ycll out "Iley, stick-man!" It's just common courtesy.

The dealers realize that many players are inex-perienced, and will be happy to help you and answer any questions.

The Boxman

In addition to the dealers, the casino employes two "boxmen" to oversee the game, each being responsible for one end of the table. They are seated at the center area of the table, across from the stickman, and directly over the casino's stash of chips. They watch the payoffs, settle disputes, count bills, and guard the game's integrity by keep-ing a close watch on the shooter, especially when the dice are in-hand.

The Floorman

The casino arranges its tables in a rectangular configuration (called a pit) and assigns one or two floormen per shift to watch over the group of tables. If any table is hot, and the casino's losing big money, the floormen will give it serious atten-tion, although there's really little they can do.

However, it's not unusual for a floorman to order new dice into a game in the hopes of chang-

ing the shooter's luck. And on occasion, they may
change the dealer's rotation prematurely, again
based more on superstition than common sense.
During a really hot shoot, I've seen all four dealers
on the stick at the order of the floorman. And on
rare occasion, I've seen a nervous floorman pester
the shooter. Some of these guys actually feel
responsible for the casino's losses.

Floormen also issue markers to credit players,
and may on occasion handle some small comps
(freebees to high rollers). But for the most part (and
this is straight from a floorman) there's not much
to do, except keep an eye on the games (and the
cocktail waitresses), smoke, and issue a few
markers. They have a cushy job, but it can be boring especially when the tables are cold as ice.

The Pit Boss

Each pit also has a pit boss who's in charge of
the entire pit. Big deal. Again, there's not much
to do. Occasionally, he'll talk on the telephone
(probably his wife telling him to bring home a loaf
of bread), also write a marker now and then, and
work the computer to check a player's credit
balance. But in big casinos, the pit boss has a girl
in the pit to do this for him. Obviously, he's too
busy with other things.

All the pit bosses report directly to the shift boss
(no kidding, another boss) who's in charge of the

entire casino for an 8-hour period. This guy
generally *is* busy. After all, he's watching the entire casino operation and gets involved with some
administrative duties.

Next up the ladder is an assistant casino
manager, then the casino manager, and still higher
is the vice-president of casino operations. The old
adage about chiefs and Indians is perfectly suited
for the casino chain-of-command. Too many
chiefs, and not enough Indians.

*This information is included to help you if you
have a dispute or problem in the casino and have
not received satisfaction.* Get on the phone and ask
the operator for the shift boss, if that doesn't work,
try the casino manager. Of course, if you still
haven't got what you wanted, you can always try
the president . . . or the board chairman . . . or
the chief executive officer . . . or . . .

THE DICE

All craps tables are about 12 to 15 inches deep,
creating a wall that's lined with sponge-rubber
shaped in a series of continuous pyramids. That's
the reason why the shooter must hit the wall when
throwing the dice. To insure a random bounce! In
addition, many of the newer tables have a cor-
rogated floor under the felt, to further insure that
the dice cannot be controlled.

The "Mechanic"

When I wrote *Pay the Line* a few years ago, I talked to many dice-pit bosses who were familiar with "mechanics." A mechanic is a shooter who tries to manipulate the outcome by his control of the dice. Some of the stories were hard to believe, but allegedly, a few players can indeed affect the frequency of certain numbers and acquire an unethical edge; not necessarily illegal because in some cases, the mechanic uses the wall to deflect the dice at precise angles.

Personally, I doubt the validity of these stories with the possible exception of one fellow who would make his throw in such a way that one dice simply slid along the table's floor (did not rotate) while the other dice tumbled behind it, creating the illusion that both dice were bouncing.

It's interesting, I'll grant you, but don't waste your time even thinking about it. Play the game fairly, and respect the casino's rules.

Dice Specifications

Casino dice are no longer made of bones, but of clear, precision-molded, plastic or polycarbonate, to the industry's rigid specifications. The dice are machined square to a tolerance of one ten-thousandth of an inch! The casino is very concerned about the strict consistency of their cubes.

When you play, you'll notice that casino dice have sharp corners, unlike the drug store variety that have radiused (rounded) corners. That's because the sharp corners create more bounce when the dice are rolled.

Incidentally, don't worry about the possibility of a major casino installing "shaved" dice. The casino advantage alone is more than enough to provide a substantial profit. There's no reason for a casino to put their priceless gaming license in jeopardy. Just to be sure, gaming control commissions in Nevada and Atlantic City will inspect casino dice without notice, removing them from any table they choose, then sealing the dice in an envelope for laboratory evaluation. But like I said, casino cheating at craps (or other games for that matter) should be the last of your worries.

The next time you pick up casino dice, look for a confidential code-number the casino uses each day to insure the dice are indeed theirs. Whenever a dice falls to the floor or whenever there's suspicion, the boxman will ask to inspect the dice, noting its condition and code-number.

By the way, the casino refers to a single dice as "dice." The term "die" although correct, isn't used.

CHAPTER 4

HOW TO BET

I'm constantly asked if I play craps, and if so, how big my bets are — as if the size of my bet is some indication of my skill, or quality of play.

The size of a player's bet has no direct bearing on his ability.

For some players, a large bet is a measure of status. Why would a player want to impress someone by making large wagers? It's not a measure of status; it's a measure of insecurity.

BET SAFELY

When I play craps, and it's not that frequently, I always begin with a $15 wager, or less if I feel like it. That certainly doesn't qualify me as a high roller! I know that the casino has a long-term advantage, so why take a large risk with a negative expectancy?

The high roller would be bored silly making a $15 bet. He needs the big bet out to feel the excitement, the tingle, the thrill of gambling. In that situation, I can only feel sorry.

I enjoy playing at the table-minimum level because it represents safe, conservative, and smart betting. That's right. **The small bets are the smart bets!**

INCREASE YOUR BETS AS YOU WIN

If I start winning with some consistency, I'll press my bets and might reach the high roller's level, but only after I'm well ahead. Basically, I'm doing what any sensible businessman would do—reinvesting my winnings (earnings) in the hopes of winning larger, future bets. But emphatically, *I'll never risk my original stake by making large bets*. A wise gambler uses only his winnings, but not all of it, in pursuit of greater profits.

Remember to keep your bets small until you start winning. Then, press up as you continue to win. *Always put some of your winnings aside to insure that you quit winners*.

Reduce your bets to the table-minimum if you start losing. Quit if it continues. *Never, under any circumstances, press a losing wager*.

A seasoned gambler always follows this classic advice: **Let the winnings run; lay back or walk away when you're losing.**

After a few winning passes at the dice tables, some players who may not have been betting boldly will ask themselves why they didn't bet heavier. Instead of betting only $5, they think what could have happened with $500, or $2,000!

Hindsight is always 20/20. How could you have known when the string of wins was about to occur? Obviously, there isn't any human way, so don't take the chance.

SHOOT-OUT AT THE MGM

This subject reminds me of the time a few years ago when I was playing at the MGM in Las Vegas, at a table filled with high rollers. The incident is hard to forget.

Three or four shooters held the dice for quite a long time. The table was red hot! There were lots of big bets out, and the floormen were worried. When the dice finally reached me, I received lots of encouragement from the other players. How could I miss under these conditions?

My first toss was a lousy 3-craps. It lost. OK, no problem. Again, I got more encouragement. "Apologize!" they shouted, "Let's see an eleven!" I threw another craps, two aces. The noise level dropped, and I got some bad stares. Another throw. Craps again! Three losers in a row.

I won't keep you in suspense. I threw two more. That's five craps in a row! But I still had the dice. The next toss was a six. Thank God! At least it wasn't another craps, and besides, a six is easy to make, right? The big bettors made their odds-bets and jumped on all the remaining place bets in an effort to recoup the losses on my come-outs. I made only my odds-bet and grabbed the dice. They bounced hard against the back-wall and came up sixty-one (6-1).

I sevened-out. Six fast losers in a row! It's a good thing it wasn't the "old days" when everyone wore guns!

Lessons from the MGM Incident

The story about the MGM dice table was nearly edited out of this book. It's really "downer" material. No one wants to hear about six losers in a row, especially when the shooter was the author they're reading. But there are so many lessons in that brief story that it had to be included.

The shooter is incidental to the game's probabilities. The fact that I was the shooter had nothing to do with the outcome. I have no control over the dice, nor do I have any reason to believe that the dice at that time didn't like me.

There's no such thing as a good shooter or a bad shooter. If you see a player at the dice tables who earlier that day had a terrific shoot, don't assume that he'll do it again. He might, but then again, he probably won't. He wasn't skilled. He was lucky. That's all.

Previous rolls have no affect on future rolls. The fact that the shooters before me had such a long success—lots of passes and lots of numbers, had absolutely no bearing on my chances. The dice have no memory.

By the same token, there is no such thing as a number being "overdue." If a shooter has thrown the dice twenty times without a 7 appearing, the dice are not "ready" for a 7 beyond their natural 1 in 6 probability. Do you actually think there's a "force" at work, urging the dice to come up 7? Think about it. The toss of dice will always produce a random event, independent of any previous results.

Winning or losing streaks are real probabilities. The odds of throwing five craps in a row is a staggering 59,048 to 1! Yet it happened. There's a much greater likelihood of throwing five 7's in a row. Any craps is an 8 to 1 probability. Any 7 is only 5 to 1. The player must be aware that, although highly unlikely, streaks of great magnitude will happen, sometime. Hopefully, you'll be there at the right time, not at the wrong time. But remember, you have no way of knowing.

When a winning streak does occur for you, I can

only hope that you will have pressed your prior winnings as you should do, and enjoy the ride!

Incidentally, pressing in this book doesn't mean doubling. It simply means increasing the size of your wager by an arbitrary amount up to perhaps 50% of your prior wager.

Learn how to quit winners. Before I "frosted" the dice, many passes were made and I had accumulated substantial winnings. Even though I had a terrible shoot to follow, *I gave little of it back*. While other players were betting heavily, as if trying to force the wins back again, I bet down. If I had continued chasing the losses, I would have ended up like the high rollers. With nothing.

Table conditions, hot or cold, have no bearing on your expectancy. Let's say that a new player had been able to squeeze in just at the time I got the dice. Knowing the table was "hot," he might have bet heavily. It would have proved disastrous. We know how it turned out.

It's also a good reason why you shouldn't begin a session with a large bet. *Let your actual winnings or losses dictate the size of your wagers*. Don't rely on "playing conditions" because it has no bearing on what you can expect. Technically, there's really no such thing as a hot table. Only a table that *was* hot. At any stage during a streak, no one can say that it's going to continue, but they can tell you how it was.

Remember, there is no scientifically sound reason for a player to worm his way into a "hot" crap table.

DANGEROUS BETTING ADVICE

As I mentioned earlier, crap games seem to attract the high rollers, more so than any other casino game, including Baccarat. Individual bets at the baccarat tables might be larger, but the quantity of wagers and the quantity of the big bettors are much greater at the dice tables.

Obviously, high rollers make big bets, and stand to win considerable money when the dice are passing. Their betting habits remind me of what an experienced dice manager at the MGM in Reno told me about winning a lot of money. He said he has a stock answer whenever anyone asks him how to win lots of money. "If you want to win thousands of dollars you have to bet thousands of dollars." He's partially right.

It's a great way to *lose* thousands of dollars also!

SMART BETTING

The bottom line on betting at the dice tables is to keep your bets relatively small (unless you're winning consistently) because the casino has the edge on every toss. Remember, the pass-line with full double-odds gives the casino a modest .6% advantage. Come-bets with full double-odds is of course the same percentage, but the place-bets, prop-bets, buy-bets, and field-bets are too much in the casino's favor to consider.

The smart player only makes pass-line and come-bets with full double-odds. That's the mark of a tough player.

If you begin with table-minimum wagers, and progress to larger bets only if you're winning, you represent the toughest opponent possible for the casino.

I don't want to give you the impression that you can make a living playing craps! You can't!

Sure, it's possible that in short-term play you might hit it big. But the more you play, the greater the chance that the casino advantage, no matter how small, will prove itself.

The casinos know that even if a player wins big, it's a temporary set-back. For most players, the game isn't over. The players will probably be back.

Even if you make only the low-percentage bets, there's an important law of probability that applies: *the longer you play, the more likely you will lose.*

BETTING "SYSTEMS"

There are hundreds of betting systems for sale to craps players, advertised in newspapers and gambling magazines. You must believe me when I tell you that no system can possibly work. *You can't change a negative expectancy into a positive expectancy by the way you bet.*

Betting progressions, as they are commonly called, have absolutely no basis of fact, and appeal only to the gullible, inexperienced player.

Other systems for sale are based on "tracking" the dice looking for numbers that haven't appeared in a given period. By now you should know that it would be a complete waste of time. Yet some people believe in it as the basis for their foolish bets.

Another system that I investigated was nothing more than a course in ESP. Can you believe it?

Unless you do have ESP, I recommend that you play just for fun, and in moderation.

Good luck!